SCRIP

P

MW00648635

Dedicated to the Memory of Pope Saint John Paul II
"The Rosary is my favorite prayer!"

Bart Tesoriero

Nihil Obstat: Reverend Francis Vivona, S.T.M., J.C.L.
Imprimatur: Most Reverend Bishop William C. Skurla, D.D.,
Bishop of the Eparchy of Van Nuys
March 25, 2006
The Annunciation of the Lord

ISBN 1-936020-71-3
Library of Congress Control Number: 2011962068

Artwork © 2006 Michael Adams • Licensee Aquinas Press
Text © 2006 Aquinas Press, Phoenix, Arizona
Printed in China

Table of Contents

INTRODUCTION

"The Rosary of the Virgin Mary...is a prayer loved by countless Saints and encouraged by the Magisterium. Simple yet profound, it still remains, at the dawn of this third millennium, a prayer of great significance, destined to bring forth a harvest of holiness." –Pope Saint John Paul II, The Rosary of the Virgin Mary

Our goal in this book is to help you receive and respond to God's grace by praying and meditating on the Scriptures surrounding the mysteries of the Rosary. Mary remembered and reflected on God's Word and actions in her life, turning them over and over in her heart. She pondered God's Word, chewing and mulling over it until it suffused and permeated her entire being. Mary treasured God's Word in her heart and lived it out in her life.

Pope Saint John Paul urges us to sit at the school of Mary and contemplate the face of Christ, so as to experience the depths of His love, a personal love for you, committed to your healing and well being, now and forever.

My Scriptural Rosary features a scripture, meditation, and response for every Hail Mary of the Rosary. As you prayerfully contemplate the saving events in the lives of Jesus and Mary, may you receive their fruit, and go forth to serve God's beloved, wounded family.

O Mary, Queen of the Most Holy Rosary, pray for us.

Our Lady, Queen of Peace, pray for us.

Meditation and the Mysteries of the Rosary

The Mysteries of the Rosary include the events surrounding Christ's Incarnation, Ministry, Passion, Death, Resurrection, Ascension, and Giving of the Holy Spirit. The final two mysteries focus on Mary's glory in heaven.

On the following pages you will find each mystery followed by a brief meditation, plus a scripture verse, meditation, and response for each Hail Mary. Every decade features at least one Old Testament scripture prophesying about or related to the mystery itself.

To meditate on the mysteries of the Rosary, reflect on each event as presented in the scriptures. Place yourself in the scene; see what the characters see, hear what they hear, be as present as possible. In so doing allow the Holy Spirit to touch your heart.

Next, apply the mystery to your own life. How does this mystery affect me? What is Jesus doing for me? What is He asking me to do? With Jesus and Mary as my models, how can I love more sincerely today? Ask God to forgive your failures and thank Him for your victories. Invite Him to transform you, through the intercession of your Mother, into the image of His Son.

Finally, as you pray each mystery, intercede for others. Stand in the gap and pray for those in the Body of Christ and in our world today who most need God's grace and favor.

The fervent prayer of a righteous person is very powerful.
–James 5:16

The Story of the Rosary

The word Rosary—*rosarium*—means of *roses*. A Rosary, then, is a *crown* of roses, with each prayer being a single rose, which we give to Mary.

Early Christian hermits daily prayed the 150 Psalms, keeping count with rocks or beads. Irish monks later divided the psalms into three groups of fifty and printed them as *The Psalter*, which enabled them to pray the Psalms communally. The *Glory Be* was always prayed with the Psalms. In time, the monks substituted the *Our Father* for each Psalm. By 1000 AD, the *Little Psalter*, a book of 150 *Our Fathers* with meditations, began to circulate.

Gradually, the *Our Fathers* were replaced with *Aves*—the angelic salutation to Mary and the greeting of Elizabeth. According to tradition, Our Lady appeared to St. Dominic in 1208 and told him to "preach my Psalter composed of 150 *Aves* and 15 *Our Fathers*." By the sixteenth century, people were meditating on the mysteries of Jesus, while praying their *Aves*.

In 1563 the Council of Trent handed down the second half of the *Hail Mary*. The *Salve Regina*, affirming Mary's role as Queen of Heaven and Earth, came next, followed by The *Apostles' Creed*. On October 7, 1573, after a miraculous naval victory at the Battle of Lepanto credited to the power of the Rosary, Pope Gregory XIII established the Feast of the Holy Rosary.

Pope Leo XIII, who shepherded the Church from 1878-1903, wrote twelve encyclicals and numerous letters on the Rosary, touching upon all its aspects and leading to a resurgence of its devotion. Through the Rosary, the pope attested, we can most quickly and easily reach Mary, and through her, Jesus.

In 1917, Mary appeared to three young children at Fatima. Referring to herself as the Lady of the Rosary, she begged all Christians to pray the Rosary daily as a powerful weapon for world peace. Mary taught the children the *Fatima Prayer*, to be prayed after the *Glory Be*.

With the heartfelt cry, **"The Family that prays together stays together!"** Father Patrick Peyton founded the Family Rosary Crusade in 1942. Father Peyton believed that world peace flowed from peace in each heart and family—and the key was family prayer, especially the Rosary.

Pope Pius XII encouraged the Family Rosary, as did his successors, most notably Pope Saint John Paul II, who wrote his apostolic letter, *The Rosary of the Virgin Mary*, in October 2002. In his letter the Pope added five new mysteries of Light—the Luminous Mysteries—to the Rosary and initiated a Year of the Rosary. Meditation on the 20 Mysteries, or scenes, from the life of Jesus and Mary remains at the heart of this time-honored and much beloved prayer to Our Lady.

The Mysteries of the Rosary

A mystery of faith is a supernatural truth that cannot be known except by God's revelation. As we pray the Rosary, a *compendium* of the Gospel, we contemplate the Christian mystery by meditating on twenty events, or mysteries, in the life of Christ and His Blessed Mother.

We pray the **Joyful Mysteries** on Mondays and Saturdays. With Mary we remember and consider the wonderful event of the Incarnation and the joy radiating from it.

We pray the **Luminous Mysteries**, the Mysteries of Light, on Thursdays. With Mary we remember and think about how Jesus, the Light of the world, proclaimed the Gospel of the Kingdom and called people to conversion during His public ministry.

We pray the **Sorrowful Mysteries** on Tuesdays and Fridays. With Mary we remember and contemplate the Passion and Death of Jesus—the fullness of the revelation of God's love. Jesus chose to give up His life so we could receive His life.

We pray the **Glorious Mysteries** on Wednesdays and Sundays. With Mary we remember and reflect on the life of the Risen Christ, the gift of the Holy Spirit, and Mary's glory in heaven. In so doing, we rediscover the reasons for our own faith and relive the joy of Mary and the disciples.

It is best to pause a moment after announcing each mystery in order to reflect on it, apply it to ourselves, and formulate an intention for it.

How to Pray the Rosary

• Make the *Sign of the Cross* and pray the *Apostles' Creed*, while holding the crucifix.
• Pray one *Our Father* on the first bead, three *Hail Marys* on the next three beads for the virtues of Faith, Hope, and Charity, and finish with a *Glory Be*.
• Announce the first Mystery. Pause for a moment to think about it. Then pray an *Our Father* on the large bead, ten *Hail Marys* on the smaller beads, and finish with a *Glory Be*. This is one decade.
• If you wish, pray the *Fatima Prayer*, found on page 11, after the *Glory Be*.
• Continue in this way until all you have prayed all five decades. To finish, pray the *Hail Holy Queen*.
• You may wish to pray the *Prayers after the Rosary*, found on page 92.

Saint Louis de Montfort's Offering of the Rosary

I unite with all the saints in Heaven, with all the just on earth and with all the faithful here present. I unite with Thee, O my Jesus, in order to praise worthily Thy holy Mother and to praise Thee in her and through her. I renounce all the distractions I may have during this Rosary, which I wish to say with modesty, attention, and devotion, just as if it were to be the last of my life.

We offer Thee, O Most Holy Trinity, this Creed in honor of all the mysteries of our Faith; this Our Father and these three Hail Marys in honor of the unity of Thy Essence and the Trinity of Thy Persons. We ask of Thee a lively faith, a firm hope and an ardent charity. Amen.

The Prayers of the Rosary

The Apostles' Creed

I believe in God, the Father Almighty,
Creator of heaven and earth; and in
Jesus Christ, His only Son, our Lord,
Who was conceived by the Holy Spirit,
born of the Virgin Mary, suffered under Pontius Pilate,
was crucified, died, and was buried.

He descended into hell; the third
day He rose from the dead.

He ascended into heaven, and is seated
at the right hand of God, the Father
Almighty; from thence He shall come
to judge the living and the dead.

I believe in the Holy Spirit, the Holy
Catholic Church, the communion
of saints, the forgiveness of sins,
the resurrection of the body, and
life everlasting. Amen.

Our Father

Our Father, Who art in heaven, hallowed be Thy Name;
Thy Kingdom come;
Thy Will be done on earth as it is in heaven.

Give us this day our daily bread;
and forgive us our trespasses,
as we forgive those who trespass against us;
and lead us not into temptation,
but deliver us from evil. Amen.

Hail Mary

Hail Mary, full of grace, the Lord is with thee;
blessed art thou among women,
and blessed is the fruit of thy womb, Jesus.

Holy Mary, Mother of God, pray for us sinners,
now and at the hour of our death. Amen.

Glory Be

Glory be to the Father, and to the Son, and to the Holy Spirit; as it was in the beginning, is now, and ever shall be, world without end. Amen.

Fatima Prayer

O my Jesus, forgive us our sins; save us from the fires of hell. Lead all souls to Heaven, especially those most in need of Your mercy.

Daily Consecration to Mary

O Mary, my Queen and my Mother, I give myself entirely to You. And as proof of my filial devotion,
I consecrate to you this day
my eyes, my ears, my mouth, my heart,
my whole being without reserve.
Wherefore, good Mother,
As I am your own,
Keep me and guard me
As your property and possession. Amen.

Prayer for the Faithful Departed

May the Souls of the Faithful Departed,
through the mercy of God, rest in peace. Amen.

The Joyful Mysteries

The Annunciation

God begins in this mystery to fulfill His promise made to our first parents after the Fall. We first meet Mary in the humble home of Nazareth, as she struggles to take in the astounding message of the Angel Gabriel. In Mary's 'Let it be,' both her own life and the lives of all humanity are forever changed, for in this most wondrous moment the Word is made flesh.

Our Father

• *In the sixth month, the angel Gabriel was sent from God to a town of Galilee called Nazareth, to a virgin betrothed to a man named Joseph, of the house of David, and the virgin's name was Mary.* –Luke 1:26-27

Meditation: In the fullness of time, when all was ready, God moved silently and swiftly, sending Gabriel to Mary with a mission that would save the world.

Response: Lord, thank You for Your faithfulness to Your Word on our behalf. Let me trust that when the time is right, You will act in my life, bringing me deliverance and salvation.

Hail Mary

- *"Hail, favored one! The Lord is with you."* –Luke 1:28

Meditation: *"'Full of grace' is the name Mary possesses in the eyes of God." –Pope Saint John Paul II*

Response: O Lord, You prepared Mary, in the silence of her heart, for her great vocation. Through her intercession, may I also trust that You favor me and are with me always.

Hail Mary

- *Then the angel said to her, "Do not be afraid, Mary, for you have found favor with God." –Luke 1:30*

Meditation: Gabriel assures Mary that she has all she needs for her mission: God and His favor.

Response: Thank You, Father, for Your favor given me in my Baptism. Help me also be not afraid to follow Jesus.

Hail Mary

- *"Behold, you will conceive in your womb and bear a son, and you shall name him Jesus." –Luke 1:31*

Meditation: Jesus, *Yeshua*, means *God saves*. All day, every day, God saves us from sin, Satan, and, yes, even ourselves. *"Who pardons all your sins, / heals all your ills." –Psalm 103:3*

Response: Jesus, You have saved me from sin and its power over me. Today, Lord, I invite You into my heart and recommit myself to You. Amen.

Hail Mary

- *"He will be great and will be called Son of the Most High, and the Lord God will give him the throne of David his father,"*
–Luke 1:32

Meditation: God fulfilled His promise to Adam and Eve, Abraham, David, and all of us in sending His Son, His final Word, to bring His Kingdom to earth.

Response: Lord, You fulfilled Your covenants of old in an awesome and astounding manner. You will also fulfill Your covenant with me, in Your Son Jesus, to give me eternal life as I trust in and follow Him.

Hail Mary

- *"and he will rule over the house of Jacob forever, and of his kingdom there will be no end."* –Luke 1:33

Meditation: Jesus will rule, not with earthly pride, power, and dominance, but with heavenly peace, mercy, and love.

Response: Lord, Your Kingdom of love is in my heart. Help me to bring Your Kingdom to others today!

Hail Mary

- *"The holy Spirit will come upon you, and the power of the Most High will overshadow you. Therefore the child to be born will be called holy, the Son of God."* –Luke 1:35

Meditation: Filled with the Holy Spirit and the power of God, Mary bore the ultimate fruit: Jesus!

Response: O Holy Spirit, come upon me this day. Fill me with Your power and love, that I too may bear Christ to the world.

Hail Mary

- *"And behold, Elizabeth, your relative, has also conceived a son in her old age, and this is the sixth month for her who was called barren; for nothing will be impossible for God."*
  –Luke 1:36-37

Meditation: Because God is Lord of all, nothing is impossible for Him.

Response: O Lord, forgive me when my faith is small. Through the prayers of Mary, help me to believe Your Word!

Hail Mary

- *Mary said, "Behold, I am the handmaid of the Lord. May it be done to me according to your word." Then the angel departed from her.* –Luke 1:38

Meditation: Just as God called Mary, He is also calling each of us, and giving us abundant grace to respond to Him.

Response: Dear Mother Mary, through your intercession, help me say yes to God in all He asks of me, with a willing heart.

Hail Mary

- *Therefore the Lord himself will give you this sign: the virgin shall be with child, and bear a son, and shall name him Immanuel.* –Isaiah 7:14

Meditation: Our God is a covenant God who keeps His promises. He reveals to Isaiah that a virgin will conceive the promised Redeemer—*God with us!*

Response: O God You gave Your very best—Your only Son—to save us. Thank You for Your faithfulness to Israel and all humanity.

Hail Mary

Glory Be

The Visitation

We travel with Mary to visit her beloved Elizabeth. Mary and Elizabeth truly love each other. Mary gives Elizabeth joy and assistance in her mission, and Elizabeth confirms and blesses Mary in hers. As we pray this mystery, Mary is near to support and strengthen us on our journey of faith.

Our Father

• *During those days Mary set out and traveled to the hill country in haste to a town of Judah, where she entered the house of Zechariah and greeted Elizabeth.* –Luke 1:39-40

Meditation: Hearing that Elizabeth was with child, Mary left immediately to visit, help, and encourage her. She forgot herself to serve others.

Response: How often do I hesitate when someone could use a hand? Today let me respond rapidly when I see a need.

Hail Mary

*• When Elizabeth heard Mary's greeting,
the infant leaped in her womb.* –Luke 1:41

Meditation: The unborn John recognizes his Messiah and Lord in Mary's womb. What God conceals from the learned, He reveals to the little ones.

Response: Lord, create in me a clean heart, that I too may see You more clearly.

Hail Mary

*• And Elizabeth, filled with the holy Spirit,
cried out in a loud voice and said,
"Most blessed are you among women,
and blessed is the fruit of your womb."* –Luke 1:41-42

Meditation: Under the anointing of the Holy Spirit, Elizabeth blesses Mary, confirming her divine visitation.

Response: Help me Lord, to rejoice in and affirm the gifts You give to others, and to fulfill my own vocation as best I can. To You be all the glory!

Hail Mary

*• "And how does this happen to me,
that the mother of my Lord should come to me?"* –Luke 1:43

Meditation: Elizabeth's humility at God's favor is a sure sign of her holiness.

Response: You alone, O Lord, are worthy of our praise. Help me to be always thankful, in awe of Your constant care for me.

Hail Mary

- *"For at the moment the sound of your greeting reached my ears, the infant in my womb leaped for joy."* –Luke 1:44

Meditation: Elizabeth exulted when she heard Mary's voice, as did her unborn child, John, when he recognized God's Son hidden in Mary.

Response: May I too recognize and rejoice in Your presence, O Lord, especially in the Holy Eucharist, where You visit us daily with the gift of Yourself!

Hail Mary

- *I rejoice heartily in the LORD, /
in my God is the joy of my soul.* –Isaiah 61:10

Meditation: Joy is our spontaneous response to God's presence—a fruit of the Holy Spirit and a delight of our human spirit.

Response: O Lord, Your joy enlivened Elizabeth. May Your joy be my strength today as well.

Hail Mary

- *"Blessed are you who believed that what was spoken to you by the Lord would be fulfilled."* –Luke 1:45

Meditation: The prophet Habakkuk stated that the just shall live by faith. Mary believed God on the strength of His Word alone, and all generations shall call her blessed.

Response: O Lord, through Mary's intercession, help me to believe more firmly in You and in the promises of Your Word.

Hail Mary

• *And Mary said: / "My soul proclaims the greatness of the Lord; / my spirit rejoices in God my savior."* –Luke 1:46-47

Meditation: Mary rejoiced first in spirit, and then with all her soul she magnified the Lord.

Response: By faith today I also rejoice in spirit, O Lord, and my soul—my whole being—will proclaim Your praise.

Hail Mary

• *"The Mighty One has done great things for me, / and holy is his name."* –Luke 1:49

Meditation: Each one of us can say this, since everything we have is a gift of the Most High. But He's not finished with us yet!

Response: Lord, as I reflect on Your wonderful gifts to me—my life, faith, and vocation—I can only thank You for doing such great things for me. Holy is Your Name!

Hail Mary

• *"He will come to us like the rain, / like spring rain that waters the earth."* –Hosea 6:3

Meditation: The Lord promised to come to His people and refresh them. In Mary's visit to her cousin He begins to fulfill His Word.

Response: Lord, thank You for coming to us through the womb of Mary, and for filling our souls with your Spirit of grace.

Hail Mary

Glory Be

The Nativity

We travel with Joseph and Mary to Bethlehem, where in the hush of this Holy Night, the Son of God is born. God gives His only Son into our hands in this marvelous mystery, as the Word becomes Flesh. The Shepherd has come to seek and save His sheep, and we will never be the same.

Our Father

• *In those days a decree went out from Caesar Augustus that the whole world should be enrolled.* –Luke 2:1

Meditation: God works through the many and varied circumstances of our life, as disconnected as they may seem at times. He is always in control.

Response: O Lord, help me to see Your hand in all situations, trusting that You are working all things together for the good.

Hail Mary

• And Joseph too went up from Galilee from the town of Nazareth to Judea, to the city of David that is called Bethlehem, because he was of the house and family of David, –Luke 2:4

Meditation: Joseph and Mary obeyed the Law, both divine and human, even when it was difficult. They continued to trust in God.

Response: O God, help me to trust and obey You even when I don't understand.

Hail Mary

• to be enrolled with Mary, his betrothed, who was with child. –Luke 2:5

Meditation: There is joy in following God, even when it's difficult, as it surely was for Mary journeying from Nazareth down to Bethlehem.

Response: Father, help me rejoice always, even when I'm hurting.

Hail Mary

• While they were there, the time came for her to have her child, and she gave birth to her firstborn son. –Luke 2:6-7

Meditation: All things have their appointed time. When all was ready, Mary gave birth to the One who would save the world.

Response: O Mary, teach me to wait upon the Lord, and to be always ready to do His Will.

Hail Mary

• *She wrapped him in swaddling clothes and laid him in a manger, because there was no room for them in the inn.*
–Luke 2:7

Meditation: From the beginning, even in the humble manger, Jesus offered Himself to us as food, the Bread of Life.

Response: Jesus, You served us from Your birth. Grant me also a servant's heart to discern and meet the needs of others.

Hail Mary

• *But you, Bethlehem-Ephrathah, / too small to be among the clans of Judah, / From you shall come forth for me / one who is to be ruler in Israel; / Whose origin is from of old, / from ancient times.* –Micah 5:1

Meditation: Long ago God spoke through the Prophet Micah foretelling the birthplace of His Son, whose origin was from eternity.

Response: Help me to hear and rely on Your Word, O Lord, even when it is prophetic or difficult to understand.

Hail Mary

• *Now there were shepherds in that region living in the fields and keeping the night watch over their flock.* –Luke 2:8

Meditation: God emptied Himself, becoming little and vulnerable, so the poor and lowly could receive Him.

Response: Forgive me, Lord, when I become proud and look down on the humble; they are the ones with whom You choose to dwell.

Hail Mary

- *The angel said to them, "Do not be afraid; for behold, I proclaim to you good news of great joy that will be for all the people."* –Luke 2:10

Meditation: God alone brings true joy, and He loves to share!

Response: Lord, how are You visiting me today? Help me to receive You with joy.

Hail Mary

- *"For today in the city of David a savior has been born for you who is Messiah and Lord."* –Luke 2:11

Meditation: God keeps His promises—abundantly! God sends us His Son as one of us—the Anointed One and Everlasting Lord.

Response: Welcome, O Infant King!

Hail Mary

"Glory to God in the highest / and on earth peace to those on whom his favor rests." –Luke 2:14

Meditation: *"The Son of God became man so that we might become God."* –Saint Athanasius

Response: Jesus, help me receive You always in the Eucharist, for Your glory, my peace, and the good of all humanity. Amen.

Hail Mary

Glory Be

The Presentation

In obedience to the Law of Moses, Mary and Joseph present Jesus to God in the temple. The long wait of Israel for the Messiah is ended. So too is the waiting of old Simeon, who blesses the Child and His parents, having been promised by the Spirit that he should not die until he had seen the Lord's Anointed One. We hear Simeon prophesy joy and sorrow for both Mother and Child, and ultimate glory for God.

Our Father

• *When the days were completed for their purification according to the law of Moses, they took him up to Jerusalem to present him to the Lord.* –Luke 2:22

Meditation: God commanded His people Israel to consecrate, or set apart, every first born male to Him, as a sign of their covenant.

Response: In Baptism I was consecrated and set apart for You, O my Lord. Today I recommit myself to You.

Hail Mary

• *and to offer the sacrifice of "a pair of turtledoves or two young*

pigeons," in accordance with the dictate in the law of the Lord.
–Luke 2:24

Meditation: Mary was already pure and Jesus was already holy, but in humility she and Joseph offer the prescribed sacrifice.

Response: Jesus, Your sacrifice has sanctified us. Help me to offer my body as a living sacrifice of praise to You.

Hail Mary

• *Now there was a man in Jerusalem whose name was Simeon. This man was righteous and devout, awaiting the consolation of Israel, and the holy Spirit was upon him.* –Luke 2:25

Meditation: Like all faithful Jews, Simeon patiently waited for God to fulfill His promises.

Response: O Lord, You call me also to wait in hope, trusting in Your perfect timing and gracious provision in everything.

Hail Mary

• *It had been revealed to him by the holy Spirit that he should not see death before he had seen the Messiah of the Lord.*
–Luke 2:26

Meditation: God gave Simeon a wonderful promise, and Simeon responded with wholehearted, expectant faith.

Response: Dear Lord, Your Word is filled with marvelous and abundant promises for us. May I, like Simeon, respond to You with expectant faith!

Hail Mary

• *He came in the Spirit into the temple;* –Luke 2:27

Meditation: God is never too late and He's never too early. He's always right on time!

Response: Lord, help me to neither get ahead of You nor fall behind You, but let me follow Your promptings today.

Hail Mary

• *and when the parents brought in the child Jesus… he took him into his arms and blessed God, saying: / "Now, Master, you may let your servant go / in peace, according to your word,"*
–Luke 2:27-29

Meditation: Simeon's mission was accomplished. He had embraced the Messiah. Now he could die in peace.

Response: Jesus, I too want to embrace You. Please bring Your peace into my heart today.

Hail Mary

• *"for my eyes have seen your salvation, / which you prepared in sight of all the peoples, / a light for revelation to the Gentiles, / and glory for your people Israel."*
–Luke 2:30-32

Meditation: God spent thousands of years preparing the world for His salvation, which would reach to the ends of the earth.

Response: Jesus, I receive *You*, the light of revelation and the glory of God *for m*e, today.

Hail Mary

• and Simeon blessed them and said to Mary his mother,
"Behold, this child is destined for the fall and rise of many in
Israel, and to be a sign that will be contradicted" –Luke 2:34

Meditation: A shadow falls across the joy of this mystery: the
Child will encounter opposition, rejection, and death.

Response: Jesus, I trust in You, even when I encounter trials and
temptations.

Hail Mary

• "(and you yourself a sword will pierce)
so that the thoughts of many hearts may be revealed."
–Luke 2:35

Meditation: Mary was willing to suffer at the foot of the Cross
so that our hearts would be open to God.

Response: Mother, help me today to take up my cross and to
follow Your Son, trusting that God will bring me to Resurrection.

Hail Mary

• Lo, I am sending my messenger / to prepare the way before me; /
And suddenly there will come to the temple / the LORD whom
you seek, / And the messenger of the covenant whom you desire.
–Malachi 3:1

Meditation: 500 years before Simeon, Malachi prophesied
Christ's coming to the temple.

Response: God, You fulfill Your promises in marvelous and
unexpected ways. Lord Jesus, let me commune with You today
in the temple of my heart!

Hail Mary

Glory Be

The Finding in the Temple

On the way home from the Passover, Mary and Joseph discover that their 12-year-old son is no longer with them. As the hours of searching turn into days, they grow more distraught. You can imagine their feelings when, after three days, they find Jesus in the Temple! We too feel confused, anxious, and depressed when we "lose" Jesus, and we cry out, "Where are you, Lord?" God is always in control, and in time, if we keep looking, we will find Jesus. Mary will lead the way.

Our Father

• *Each year his parents went to Jerusalem for the feast of Passover, and when he was twelve years old, they went up according to festival custom.*
–Luke 2:41-42

Meditation: Joseph, Mary, and Jesus participated fully in Israel's liturgical life and worship.

Response: Thank You, Lord, for inviting me to actively enter in to the liturgical and sacramental life of Your Church, the new Israel.

Hail Mary

• *After they had completed its days, as they were returning, the boy Jesus remained behind in Jerusalem, but his parents did not know it.* –Luke 2:43

Meditation: The Spirit blows where it wills, and we know not where or when He will lead us.

Response: Lord, help me to listen and respond to the promptings of Your Spirit.

Hail Mary

• *Thinking that he was in the caravan, they journeyed for a day and looked for him among their relatives and acquaintances, but not finding him, they returned to Jerusalem to look for him.* –Luke 2:44-45

Meditation: Joseph and Mary were really distressed—they had lost the center of their life and the light of their hearts!

Response: Jesus, when we are separated physically, spiritually, or emotionally from loved ones, reunite us through Your love.

Hail Mary

• *After three days they found him in the temple, sitting in the midst of the teachers, listening to them and asking them questions.* –Luke 2:46

Meditation: What a relief! Jesus is found—but why did He leave us?

Response: Lord, many times I don't understand You or Your ways. Even so, help me trust that You always know best!

Hail Mary

• *All who heard him were astounded at his understanding and his answers.* –Luke 2:47

Meditation: The Teacher taught the teachers, and they were spellbound.

Response: Lord, there is so much more to You than I know. May I always be open to Your precious Spirit!

Hail Mary

• *When his parents saw him, they were astonished, and his mother said to him, "Son, why have you done this to us? Your father and I have been looking for you with great anxiety."* –Luke 2:48

Meditation: Mary and Joseph felt astonished, anxious, and angry when they finally tracked down their son. Surely a lot of parents can relate!

Response: God, Your ways are not our ways. Thank You that I can share my feelings with You when I don't comprehend.

Hail Mary

• *And he said to them, "Why were you looking for me? Did you not know that I must be in my Father's house?"* –Luke 2:49

Meditation: Jesus expected His parents to know that God would always take first place in His life.

Response: May my heart, O Lord, be always set on You.

Hail Mary

• *But they did not understand what he said to them.* –Luke 2:50

Meditation: Joseph and Mary didn't grasp Jesus' meaning and the veiled reference to his Passion, Death, and Resurrection.

Response: Lord, like Joseph and Mary, many times I don't understand Your Word or ways. Help me to walk by faith until Your light dawns in my heart.

Hail Mary

• *He went down with them and came to Nazareth, and was obedient to them; and his mother kept all these things in her heart.* –Luke 2:51

Meditation: In obedience to His parents, Jesus left the temple and returned home, to remain there until the Spirit would lead Him forth for His mission.

Response: Mary, help me both to obey God and to reflect prayerfully on the events of my life, that I may see His purpose in all I experience.

Hail Mary

• *"A prophet like me will the LORD, your God, raise up for you from among your own kinsmen; to him you shall listen."* –Deuteronomy 18:15

Meditation: Even in His youth, Jesus fulfills God's promise of a Prophet who would teach all who would listen.

Response: Open my heart, Lord, and teach me to listen to You.

Hail Mary

Glory Be

The Luminous Mysteries

The Baptism of Jesus

 Jesus, now 30 years of age, leaves Nazareth and journeys to the Jordan, to be baptized by John. After His baptism, the heavens are torn asunder, God affirms His Beloved Son, and the fullness of the Spirit rests upon Him. Jesus accepts His mission as God's Suffering Servant, fulfilling Isaiah's prophecy, and is manifested to Israel. His mission has begun.

Our Father

• *A man named John was sent from God.* –John 1:6

Meditation: God is the Divine Initiator. As Master of the Universe, He sets the plan of salvation in motion.

Response: Help me, dear Lord, to discern and fulfill *my* role in Your plan of salvation.

Hail Mary

• *He came for testimony, to testify to the light,*
so that all might believe through him. –John 1:7

Meditation: God sent John to awaken the heart and conscience of Israel by bearing witness to the coming Light of Christ.

Response: Dear God, awaken my heart to desire all You have for me—the fullness of Your Spirit and the growth of Your Kingdom in my life.

Hail Mary

• *As it is written in Isaiah the prophet: / "Behold, I am sending my messenger ahead of you; / he will prepare your way."*
–Mark 1:2

Meditation: God always prepares the ground before He sends His seed. John the Baptist fulfills Isaiah's ancient prophecy, and readies the soil of Israel.

Response: Thank You Lord, for preparing my heart to receive Jesus, even when I don't always recognize Your hand in my life.

Hail Mary

• *"A voice of one crying out in the desert: /*
'Prepare the way of the Lord, / make straight his paths.' "
–Mark 1:3

Meditation: John's message is urgent: The God Man is coming, and we must get ready.

Response: Jesus, help me prepare my heart to receive Your Spirit. May Your Will be done in me.

Hail Mary

• *And this is what he proclaimed: "One mightier than I is coming after me. I am not worthy to stoop and loosen the thongs of his sandals." –Mark 1:7*

Meditation: Humility is truth. John realized that he was only the messenger for Christ, the Son of the Living God.

Response: O God, forgive me for not appreciating You for Who You are. You are Holy, the Lord God Almighty!

Hail Mary

• *"I have baptized you with water; he will baptize you with the holy Spirit." –Mark 1:8*

Meditation: John baptized with water from the earth; Jesus will baptize with fire from heaven.

Response: Come, Holy Spirit! Fill the hearts of Your faithful, and kindle in us the fire of Your divine love!

Hail Mary

• *It happened in those days that Jesus came from Nazareth of Galilee and was baptized in the Jordan by John. –Mark 1:9*

Meditation: Jesus, the Lamb of God, identifies Himself with sinners, and is baptized. As He enters the Jordan, Jesus anticipates His "baptism" of suffering.

Response: Jesus, You love me so much that You took on my humanity and identified with my sin. You will never let me go.

Hail Mary

• *On coming up out of the water he saw the heavens being torn open and the Spirit, like a dove, descending upon him.*
–Mark 1:10

Meditation: God the Father unlocked the heavens, closed since Adam's Fall, to reveal Jesus as Messiah and Beloved Son.

Response: Jesus, You are the new Adam, the source of the Spirit for all humanity. Fill me today with Your Power!

Hail Mary

• *And a voice came from the heavens, "You are my beloved Son; with you I am well pleased."* –Mark 1:11

Meditation: God shows His full delight in His Son who has accepted His mission.

Response: O God, only You can accomplish Your work in me. Help me to accept my mission, with its joys and sufferings, and to do Your Will.

Hail Mary

• *"Now I have seen and testified that he is the Son of God."*
–John 1:34

Meditation: After our Baptism, "the Holy Spirit swoops down upon us…and…we become sons of God." –*Saint Hilary of Poitiers*

Response: Jesus, I rejoice in the new life You give me every day. Protect me from sin, that I may walk in Your Spirit always.

Hail Mary

Glory Be

The Wedding at Cana

 At Mary's request, Jesus works His first miracle, displaying God's generous provision by changing water into enough wine for several weddings. He opens the hearts of His disciples to faith, to which we are all called in the proclamation of the Kingdom. Mary notices the needs of others and commends them to Jesus— shouldn't we do the same? When we bring our needs to Mary, she will take care of them with her Son.

Our Father

• *On the third day there was a wedding in Cana in Galilee, and the mother of Jesus was there. Jesus and his disciples were also invited to the wedding.* –John 2:1-2

Meditation: Jesus chooses a wedding as the site of His first miracle, revealing God's delight in the union of husband and wife, itself a sign of divine love.

Response: Lord Jesus, Your presence brings us new joy and new life. I receive them both from You today with a grateful heart.

Hail Mary

• *When the wine ran short, the mother of Jesus said to him, "They have no wine." –John 2:3*

Meditation: *"To be merciful is to have a heart distressed at the distress of another." –Saint Thomas Aquinas*

Response: O Mary, help me to love with your heart, always concerned for the needs of others.

Hail Mary

• *[And] Jesus said to her, "Woman, how does your concern affect me? My hour has not yet come." –John 2:4*

Meditation: Jesus recognized in Mary's request His Father's prompting of mercy for humanity, which would eventually lead to His "hour" of suffering. He put the choice in Mary's hands.

Response: God, You have given me the power to choose the good. O Mary, help me to do it!

Hail Mary

• *His mother said to the servers, "Do whatever he tells you." –John 2:5*

Meditation: Mary makes her decision—to serve others, knowing it will lead to the death of her only Son.

Response: Mary, you gave everything for us. Help us to follow your example, and to do whatever Jesus tells us.

Hail Mary

• *Now there were six stone water jars there for Jewish ceremonial washings,*
each holding twenty to thirty gallons. –John 2:6

Meditation: The Old Law commanded ritual washing as a sign of Israel's need for purification. Jesus used the jars of the Old Covenant to make the wine of the New!

Response: O Lord, exchange my hardened, judgmental heart for a new one of mercy and compassion.

Hail Mary

• *Jesus told them, "Fill the jars with water."*
So they filled them to the brim. –John 2:7

Meditation: In obedience to Jesus, the servants do their task. Their faith shall be rewarded.

Response: O Lord, help me to obey You promptly, even when I don't understand. Jesus, I trust in You.

Hail Mary

• *Then he told them, "Draw some out now and take it to the headwaiter." So they took it. –John 2:8*

Meditation: The obedient servants witness firsthand Jesus' astounding miracle!

Response: Jesus, You cannot be outdone in generosity or confidence. Help me step out in obedient faith today.

Hail Mary

> • *And when the headwaiter tasted the water that had become wine…the headwaiter called the bridegroom and said to him, "Everyone serves good wine first…but you have kept the good wine until now."* –John 2:9-10

Meditation: The New Covenant begins as the ritual waters of the Law are changed into the liberating wine of the Spirit.

Response: God, You are amazing! Thank You for transforming me into good wine for others.

Hail Mary

> • *Jesus did this as the beginning of his signs in Cana in Galilee and so revealed his glory, and his disciples began to believe in him.* –John 2:11

Meditation: Jesus' miracle "makes manifest the fulfillment of the wedding feast in the Father's kingdom, where the faithful will drink the new wine…the Blood of Christ." –*Catechism of the Catholic Church, par. 1335.*

Response: O Lord, help us to often receive this new wine, Your Blood, given for us in the Eucharist.

Hail Mary

> • *The people who walked in darkness / have seen a great light; Upon those who dwelt in the land of gloom / a light has shone.* –Isaiah 9:1

Meditation: Jesus fulfills ancient prophecy in bringing light through His first miracle in Cana of Galilee.

Response: O Lord, through Your Spirit, help us to turn the water of this day's life into the wine of gladness and joy!

Hail Mary

Glory Be

The Proclamation of the Kingdom

 Jesus preaches in the synagogues, streets, and hills of Israel, offering individuals the fulfillment of all their hopes and dreams. People listen spellbound as He tells them how to enter the kingdom: "Repent, turn around, and believe the Good News!" Jesus is knocking on the door of our hearts. We too must repent and believe, that He is the answer, the One who will lead us to true and complete freedom.

Our Father

• *After John had been arrested, Jesus came to Galilee proclaiming the gospel of God.* –Mark 1:14

Meditation: John has prepared the way; the moment has come. Jesus proclaims the Kingdom!

Response: Lord, You have prepared the ground of my heart. Help me receive Your Kingdom today.

Hail Mary

> *As he passed by the Sea of Galilee, he saw Simon and his brother Andrew casting their nets into the sea; they were fishermen. Jesus said to them, "Come after me, and I will make you fishers of men."*
> –Mark 1:16-17

Meditation: We must convert to enter the Kingdom. Simon and Andrew had a choice to make. Thank God they chose wisely!

Response: Dear God, how many times have You called my name? Help me today to respond with a heartfelt, "Here I am, Lord."

Hail Mary

> *Then they abandoned their nets and followed him.*
> –Mark 1:18

Meditation: Andrew and Simon abandoned their past to follow Jesus. From then on, they would use their nets for God's glory.

Response: Dear God, You gave me my talents and abilities. I surrender them to You. Help me use them for the Kingdom.

Hail Mary

> *The people were astonished at his teaching, for he taught them as one having authority and not as the scribes.* –Mark 1:22

Meditation: Jesus proclaimed the Gospel with authority, making an absolute claim on his listeners, as did the prophets of old.

Response: O Lord, Your Word rings true to my heart. Let me hear Your Gospel with fresh ears and a new heart, for it is the power of God unto salvation.

Hail Mary

• *They came bringing to him a paralytic carried by four men.*
—Mark 2:3

Meditation: God rewards expectant, trusting faith. The friends of the paralytic seized their moment of opportunity and brought their friend to the Lord.

Response: Lord, please grant me faith the size of a mustard seed, that I too may see the works of God.

Hail Mary

• *Unable to get near Jesus because of the crowd, they opened up the roof above him. After they had broken through, they let down the mat on which the paralytic was lying.* –Mark 2:4

Meditation: These men were not only expectant, they were determined! *"God never withholds Himself from the soul that perseveres."* –Saint Teresa of Avila

Response: O God, You are closer to me right now than my very breath. Help me seek You until Your love breaks through!

Hail Mary

• *When Jesus saw their faith, he said to the paralytic, "Child, your sins are forgiven."* –Mark 2:5

Meditation: *"Jesus proclaims the coming of the Kingdom of God, calls to conversion, and forgives the sins of all who draw near to him in humble trust."* –Pope Saint John Paul II

Response: O Lord, I feel overwhelmed by my failures and sins. Thank You forever for Your forgiveness which I receive over and over again in the sacrament of Reconciliation.

Hail Mary

• He said to the paralytic, "I say to you, rise, pick up your mat, and go home." –Mark 2:11

Meditation: Jesus first unbinds the paralytic's soul, and then his body. He goes home a new man!

Response: O God, is there anything too hard for You? I just praise You for your unbelievable goodness to the children of men.

Hail Mary

• He rose, picked up his mat at once, and went away in the sight of everyone. They were all astounded and glorified God, saying, "We have never seen anything like this." –Mark 2:12

• Meditation: From His birth to His death, and everywhere in between, Jesus' obedience glorifies His Father.

Response: Lord, I too want to glorify You today. Help me follow You with expectant faith and ready obedience.

Hail Mary

• The spirit of the Lord GOD is upon me, / because the LORD has anointed me; / He has sent me to bring glad tidings to the lowly, / to heal the brokenhearted, / To proclaim liberty to the captives / and release to the prisoners. –Isaiah 61:1

Meditation: Anointed by the Spirit, Jesus fulfills Isaiah's thrilling prophecy, bringing God's Kingdom to all through His preaching, healing, deliverance, and forgiveness of sins.

Response: Jesus, help me to seek first Your Kingdom in my life, that I may walk in freedom and joy as God's beloved child!

Hail Mary

Glory Be

The Transfiguration

The Transfiguration is *par excellence* the mystery of light as Jesus reveals His divinity to His disciples, preparing them for the sorrow of His Passion and the triumph of His Resurrection. It is a sign of the transformation that God wants to work in us as well. *"All of us, gazing with unveiled face on the glory of the Lord, are being transformed into the same image from glory to glory, as from the Lord who is the Spirit."*
–2 Corinthians 3:18

Our Father

• *After six days Jesus took Peter, James, and John his brother, and led them up a high mountain by themselves.*
–Matthew 17:1

Meditation: Just as Moses climbed Mount Sinai and Elijah went up Mount Horeb, so Peter, James, and John follow Jesus up Mount Tabor, in preparation for His ascent of Mount Cavalry.

Response: Lord, help me to follow You through the mountains and valleys of my life, trusting You in both joy and sorrow to lead me to the Father's House.

Hail Mary

• *And he was transfigured before them; his face shone like the sun and his clothes became white as light.* –Matthew 17:2

Meditation: For a moment, Jesus allows His divinity to shine through His humanity, as He radiates the glory of the only-begotten Son of God.

Response: Lord, may I too reflect Your glory as the light of the world.

Hail Mary

• *And behold, Moses and Elijah appeared to them, conversing with him.* –Matthew 17:3

Meditation: Moses, Giver of the Law, and Elijah, Israel's greatest Prophet, together represent the entire Old Covenant.

Response: Lord, the Law and the Prophets announced Your suffering and subsequent glory. Help me to bear my cross patiently, in the confident hope of entering Your Kingdom.

Hail Mary

• *Then Peter said to Jesus in reply, "Lord, it is good that we are here. If you wish, I will make three tents here, one for you, one for Moses, and one for Elijah."* –Matthew 17:4

Meditation: Whenever God reveals Himself, the response is absolute awe. *"For our God is a consuming fire."* –Hebrews 12:29

Response: O God, thank You for revealing Your glory in what is seen and unseen. Keep me close to You, O Lord!

Hail Mary

• *While he was still speaking, behold, a bright cloud cast a shadow over them,* –Matthew 17:5

Meditation: *"The whole Trinity appeared: the Father in the voice; the Son in the man; the Spirit in the shining cloud."* –Saint Thomas Aquinas

Response: Lord, Your Transfiguration is a foretaste of Your glorious coming, when You will make our bodies like Your own in glory, if only we suffer with You, so as to reign with You.

Hail Mary

• *then from the cloud came a voice that said, "This is my beloved Son, with whom I am well pleased; listen to him."* –Matthew 17:5

Meditation: In Jesus' Baptism, His heavenly Father spoke to Him. In the Transfiguration, God speaks to us: *Listen to Him!*

Response: Lord Jesus, Your Father echoes Mary's direction to the wedding servants at Cana. Help us to listen to You and do whatever You tell us.

Hail Mary

• *When the disciples heard this, they fell prostrate and were very much afraid. But Jesus came and touched them, saying, "Rise, and do not be afraid."* –Matthew 17:6-7

Meditation: Though He is an awesome God, the Father gives us Jesus so we can approach Him in peace and confidence.

Response: O God, today I put my trust in You. Help me to be not afraid regardless of what I may encounter, for You are *"an ever-present help in distress."* –Psalm 46:2

Hail Mary

• *And when the disciples raised their eyes, they saw no one else but Jesus alone.* –Matthew 17:8

Meditation: In the Transfiguration, Jesus rewarded Peter, James, and John for prayerfully and faithfully following Him, and at the same time prepared them for their ministry as servant leaders.

Response: Please send Your Spirit upon me, Lord, that I too may "see You more clearly, love You more dearly, and follow You more nearly, day by day."

Hail Mary

• *As they were coming down from the mountain, Jesus charged them, "Do not tell the vision to anyone until the Son of Man has been raised from the dead."* –Matthew 17:9

Meditation: Jesus is a Son who will be obedient unto death, and then will be raised to reign forever.

Response: Jesus, I find myself wanting Your glory while avoiding Your Cross, yet You show me that both are necessary if we are going to win the victory with You.

Hail Mary

• *I will proclaim the decree of the LORD, / who said to me, "You are my son; / today I am your father."* –Psalm 2:7

Meditation: Jesus fulfills David's Psalm, as the true Son who will carry out the Father's Will and win salvation for humanity.

Response: Lord, may Your presence in my life help me carry my cross and come with You to the joy of the Resurrection and a life transfigured by Your Spirit. Amen.

Hail Mary

Glory Be

The Institution of the Eucharist

As the apostles gather in the Holy City for Israel's most solemn and ancient feast, Jesus suddenly changes the ritual. He proclaims that the bread and wine are now His Body and Blood, given for the salvation of all, so that He can be with us forever. "In the Eucharist Jesus gives to us his body and blood, testifying to the end his love for all humanity, for whose salvation he will offer himself in sacrifice." *–Pope Saint John Paul II, The Rosary of the Virgin Mary*

Our Father

• *Before the feast of Passover, Jesus knew that his hour had come to pass from this world to the Father. He loved his own in the world and he loved them to the end.* –John 13:1

Meditation: Jesus, realizing his hour had come, gave us the Eucharist so that He would never depart from us and to make us "sharers in his Passover." *–Catechism of the Catholic Church, par. 1337*

Response: Jesus, You died so You could always be with me, especially in the Eucharist. Help me to receive You often into my heart, so I can always be with You!

Hail Mary

- *When it was evening, he reclined at table with the Twelve.*
  –Matthew 26:20

Meditation: The Twelve—Jesus' closest disciples, expecting the triumphant reign of the Messiah—gathered to celebrate the Passover with their beloved leader.

Response: Dear Jesus, thank You for the intimacy I share with family and friends, especially at meals. Stay with us always!

Hail Mary

- *Then he took the bread, said the blessing, broke it, and gave it to them, saying, "This is my body, which will be given for you; do this in memory of me."* –Luke 22:19

Meditation: Jesus, the Passover Lamb of the New Covenant, freely gives up His Body for the life of the world.

Response: Lord, You gave up Your Body for me. Help me give up my body for You.

Hail Mary

- *Then he took a cup, gave thanks, and gave it to them, saying, "Drink from it, all of you, for this is my blood of the covenant, which will be shed on behalf of many for the forgiveness of sins."* –Matthew 26:27-28

Meditation: Just as the blood of the Passover lamb saved Israel from death, the blood of Jesus saves us from our sins.

Response: *How can I repay the LORD / for all the good done for me? / I will raise the cup of salvation / and call on the name of the LORD.* –Psalm 116:12-13

Hail Mary

- *"Amen, I say to you, I shall not drink again the fruit of the vine until the day when I drink it new in the kingdom of God."*
  –Mark 14:25

Meditation: In the Eucharist, Jesus foresees the day when we will be gathered into heaven with Him forever, in the wedding feast of the Lamb.

Response: Jesus, I feel sad for You, for the suffering and loneliness ahead in Your Passion. Yet I also look forward, with You, to Your reign of love.

Hail Mary

- *"I no longer call you slaves, because a slave does not know what his master is doing. I have called you friends, because I have told you everything I have heard from my Father."*
  –John 15:15

Meditation: The Father held nothing back from Jesus, and Jesus holds nothing back from us.

Response: Lord, You call me to share Your love with the world. Help me to go forth and bear fruit for You!

Hail Mary

- *"I give you a new commandment: love one another. As I have loved you, so you also should love one another."* –John 13:34

Meditation: All our successes are successes of love, and all our failures are failures to love.

Response: O God, please help me to love others with Your love.

Hail Mary

- *"This is how all will know that you are my disciples, if you have love for one another."* –John 13:35

Meditation: The only way the world will know we belong to Him, is if we love.

Response: Lord, I am available. Change my heart, O God!

Hail Mary

- *Then, after singing a hymn, they went out to the Mount of Olives.* –Matthew 26:30

Meditation: The Passover ended with Psalms sung in praise to God. Thus Israel worshipped God as Jesus prepared for the Sacrifice.

Response: Lord, You instruct us to praise You always and everywhere. I praise You now, my Lord and My God!

Hail Mary

- *For from the rising of the sun, even to its setting, /
my name is great among the nations; /
And everywhere they bring sacrifice to my name, /
and a pure offering; /
For great is my name among the nations, /
says the LORD of hosts.* –Malachi 1:11

Meditation: Jesus fulfilled Malachi's prophecy in this first Eucharist, which has been repeated endlessly, from the rising to the setting of the sun.

Response: Lord, Your Word is perfect. We thank You for Your Body and Blood, Soul and Divinity, given to us in the Eucharist. May Your Kingdom come. Amen.

Hail Mary

Glory Be

The Sorrowful Mysteries

The Agony in the Garden

 As His closest friends sleep, Jesus enters alone the extreme agony, fear, and distress of this night of sorrow. Desiring to be spared such great suffering, Jesus prays, "Abba, Father, all things are possible to You. Take this cup away from Me, yet not My Will, but Yours, be done." Jesus pours out His anguished heart, begging for the strength to endure the Passion and finish the cup. He places His full trust and confidence in His Heavenly Father, as He had His whole life. And in His Father's embrace He finds the strength to go on to the end. Jesus teaches us that we too find our ultimate fulfillment only in giving of ourselves to others.

Our Father

- *Then going out he went, as was his custom, to the Mount of Olives, and the disciples followed him.* –Luke 22:39

Meditation: Just as Adam turned from God in a Garden, so now Jesus enters the Garden of Gethsemane to reverse Adam's disobedience and to redeem all humanity from the curse of sin and death.

Response: Lord Jesus, though You were sinless, You willingly accepted the sin of the whole world to free me from eternal death. How can I thank You?

Hail Mary

• When he arrived at the place he said to them,
"Pray that you may not undergo the test." –Luke 22:40

Meditation: Jesus exhorts His apostles to pray for the strength to do God's Will as the Enemy approaches.

Response: Lord, forgive me for the many times I have ignored Your Spirit's promptings. Help me to pray daily, that I may always overcome evil with good.

Hail Mary

• After withdrawing about a stone's throw from them and kneeling, he prayed, saying, "Father, if you are willing, take this cup away from me; still, not my will but yours be done."
–Luke 22:41-42

Meditation: As a human, Jesus felt the sorrow and horror that death represents. Even so, He unites His will completely to His Father's, and embraces suffering out of love for us.

Response: Lord, too often I take the easy way out. I don't choose Your Will because it is difficult. Help me to surrender my will to Yours, knowing it will result in true happiness.

Hail Mary

• [And to strengthen him an angel from heaven appeared to him.] –Luke 22:43

Meditation: In His temptation in the desert, angels ministered to Jesus. Now the Father sends an angel to help Jesus as the devil begins his final, frontal assault.

Response: Thank You, O God, for creating angels, who assist us in many hidden and wonderful ways. With their heavenly aid, may we please You always.

Hail Mary

• *[He was in such agony and he prayed so fervently that his sweat became like drops of blood falling on the ground.]* –Luke 22:44

Meditation: Adam was cursed after the Fall with "the sweat of his brow." Now Jesus sweats blood for us, to redeem us from the curse of sin.

Response: When my suffering and temptation seem unbearable, let me remember that Jesus has borne it for me, and I can rest in Him.

Hail Mary

• *When he rose from prayer and returned to his disciples, he found them sleeping from grief.* –Luke 22:45

Meditation: When we are distressed or broken-hearted, we seek the comfort of family and friends. Imagine Jesus' lonely sorrow as His apostles let Him down in His hour of need.

Response: O Jesus, help me to visit You often in the Blessed Sacrament and to be present to others in their hour of need, with Your loving grace!

Hail Mary

• *He said to them, "Why are you sleeping? Get up and pray that you may not undergo the test."* –Luke 22:46

Meditation: God calls me daily to pray, to abide in Him, to commune with Him. Time with Him is our greatest treasure.

Response: Lord Jesus, forgive me for the times I have let You down. Give me the fortitude to follow always the promptings of Your Holy Spirit.

Hail Mary

- *While he was still speaking… Judas…went up to Jesus to kiss him. Jesus said to him, "Judas, are you betraying the Son of Man with a kiss?"* –Luke 22:47-48

Meditation: There is no sorrow like the rejection of a friend. Yet, how many times have I rejected the Lord, my Best Friend?

Response: Dear Jesus, forgive me for the times I choose my will over Yours, and push You away from me. Draw me back to You, O Lord, and fill me with Your love and grace.

Hail Mary

- *"Even the friend who had my trust, / who shared my table, has scorned me."* –Psalm 41:10

Meditation: Judas unwittingly fulfills the Scripture in his betrayal of Jesus.

Response: Lord, how often have I betrayed You by my actions? Even so, You have forgiven me and given me another chance. Heal me, O Lord, that I may serve You.

Hail Mary

- *Like water my life drains away; / all my bones grow soft. / My heart has become like wax, / it melts away within me.* –Psalm 22:15

Meditation: King David prophesies of Jesus' suffering, as He accepts the Father's Will in His passion and death, which will lead to His Glorious Resurrection!

Response: Jesus, You did for us what we could not do for ourselves, and You did it out love. I receive You in my heart today. Thank You!

Hail Mary

Glory Be

The Scourging at the Pillar

After being betrayed, falsely accused, and wrongfully imprisoned, Jesus is handed over to the Gentiles for sentencing. His first punishment is a merciless scourging from the Roman soldiers, in which He suffers intense, unbearable pain. In His scourging, Jesus is thinking of you.

How do I respond to pain? Do I complain and give in to self-pity, or do I seek to bear it bravely, joining my sufferings to Christ's for the sake of others?

Our Father

• *As soon as morning came, the chief priests with the elders and the scribes...bound Jesus, led him away, and handed him over to Pilate.* –Mark 15:1

Meditation: After Jesus' arrest and mock trial in the dead of night, the religious leaders brought Jesus to Pilate, since they could not execute Him themselves.

Response: Jesus, I feel saddened and angry when I am snubbed or ill-treated. Help me to remember that You will never reject me.

Hail Mary

• *Now on the occasion of the feast the governor was accustomed to release to the crowd one prisoner whom they wished.*
–Matthew 27:15

Meditation: Pilate, realizing Jesus' innocence, looked for a way to release Him.

Response: Jesus, help me to speak up for the innocent—the unborn, elderly, and afflicted— who cannot speak for themselves.

Hail Mary

• *So when they had assembled, Pilate said to them, "Which one do you want me to release to you, [Jesus] Barabbas, or Jesus called Messiah?"* –Matthew 27:17

Meditation: Pilate offers the people a choice between Barabbas (son of the father), who represents rebellion, violence, and revenge, and Jesus (Son of the Father), who represents obedience, mercy, and forgiveness.

Response: Dear Jesus, I also must choose between Your way and the world's way. Help me today to live a life worthy of You.

Hail Mary

• *For he knew that it was out of envy that they had handed him over.* –Matthew 27:18

Meditation: Pilate saw through the false charges into the hearts of the chief priests and scribes. They envied Jesus—His freedom, His power, and His popularity—and so they sought to do away with Him.

Response: I too am tempted to envy those who seem better off than myself. Help me to realize, Lord Jesus, that You love and have a special plan for each one of us!

Hail Mary

• *The chief priests and the elders persuaded the crowds to ask for Barabbas but to destroy Jesus.* –Matthew 27:20

Meditation: Those who lead have a serious responsibility to guide wisely. Here the religious leaders make a tragic mistake.

Response: Lord, please give me today the fortitude to stand up for the truth, whether it is convenient or inconvenient.

Hail Mary

• *Pilate said to them, "Then what shall I do with Jesus called Messiah?" They all said, "Let him be crucified!"* –Matthew 27:22

Meditation: Out of fear, Pilate abdicates his responsibility and puts Jesus' fate into the hands of the people.

Response: O Lord, how often I have failed You and others out of fear! When I am weak, may Your power be strong in me. I pray for perseverance.

Hail Mary

• *When Pilate saw that he was not succeeding at all, but that a riot was breaking out instead, he took water and washed his hands in the sight of the crowd, saying, "I am innocent of this man's blood. Look to it yourselves."* –Matthew 27:24

Meditation: Pilate gives in to pressure and condemns a just man.

Response: How often do I protest my innocence in a matter while in my heart I know I am at least partially to blame? Cleanse me from my hidden faults, O God.

Hail Mary

• And the whole people said in reply, "His blood be upon us and upon our children." –Matthew 27:25

Meditation: Israel was God's special possession. He loved His people, and loves them still, with an everlasting love. Their heartbreaking rejection of Jesus serves as a warning for us all to stay close to God.

Response: O Jesus, forgive me for the times I have taken Your love for granted, and done my will instead of Yours. I too am responsible for Your death.

Hail Mary

• Then he released Barabbas to them, but after he had Jesus scourged, he handed him over to be crucified. –Matthew 27:26

Meditation: Jesus endured the excruciating pain of the scourging out of love for us, so passionate was His desire to be with us forever.

Response: Jesus, Your suffering gives me the power to resist sin and choose You. Make me Yours forever, O valiant Friend!

Hail Mary

• But he was pierced for our offenses, / crushed for our sins, / Upon him was the chastisement that makes us whole, / by his stripes we were healed. –Isaiah 53:5

Meditation: Jesus fulfills the Suffering Servant prophecy of Isaiah. Through His sacrifice we are healed and made whole.

Response: Jesus, You proved Your love for me in the Scourging at the Pillar. Help me to follow You always. Amen.

Hail Mary

Glory Be

The Crowning With Thorns

 Hundreds of rough Roman soldiers strip Jesus of His blood soaked clothing and throw a scarlet military cloak over His shoulders. They then press down a crown of spiked thorns on His head, striking Him and mocking Him, saying, "All hail, King of the Jews!" Jesus courageously and silently endures this humiliation out of great love and even gladly, for our salvation and that of the whole world.

Our Father

• *Then the soldiers of the governor took Jesus inside the praetorium and gathered the whole cohort around him.*
–Matthew 27:27

Meditation: A cohort—up to 600 soldiers—gathered in Pilate's official residence to mock the "King of the Jews".

Response: Jesus, everything about Your Passion was unjust. Even so, You bore it silently and with dignity. Help me to be strong and true when I am humiliated.

Hail Mary

• They stripped off his clothes and threw a scarlet military cloak about him. –Matthew 27:28

Meditation: The soldiers tried to shame Jesus, but He was not ashamed to suffer for them, and us.

Response: Jesus, for my sake, You were not ashamed of embarrassment; help me to willingly and honestly confess my sins, and amend my life, for You.

Hail Mary

• Weaving a crown out of thorns, they placed it on his head, and a reed in his right hand. –Matthew 27:29

Meditation: Jesus, now mortally wounded by the horrific crown and made to look like a fool, continued to love those who mocked Him.

Response: Jesus, I feel angry when I am mocked or insulted, especially by those close to me. Help me to live for You!

Hail Mary

• And kneeling before him, they mocked him, saying, "Hail, King of the Jews!" –Matthew 27:29

Meditation: Little did the soldiers realize, as they knelt before Jesus, that they were in fact speaking the truth. He was, and is, the King of the Jews and Master of the Universe.

Response: Dear Jesus, someday every knee shall bend before You, and every tongue proclaim, to the glory of God the Father, that You truly are Lord. Praise God!

Hail Mary

• They spat upon him and took the reed and kept striking him on the head. –Matthew 27: 30

Meditation: Jesus endured unimaginable humiliation and torture to gain the prize of everlasting life for us all.

Response: Jesus, You willingly suffered ridicule for me. May I be not afraid when I am ridiculed for You.

Hail Mary

• So Jesus came out, wearing the crown of thorns and the purple cloak. And he said to them, "Behold, the man!" –John 19:5

Meditation: Pilate brought Jesus out, scourged, beaten, crowned with thorns, covered with spittle, and clothed in a soldier's cloak. *"Ecce Homo—Behold the Man!"*

Response: Jesus, as You stood before the crowd You revealed the love of God, Who humbled Himself to save us, and the meaning of man, who is fulfilled in serving God and others.

Hail Mary

• When the chief priests and the guards saw him they cried out, "Crucify him, crucify him!" Pilate said to them, "Take him yourselves and crucify him. I find no guilt in him." –John 19:6

Meditation: Pilate had hoped that Jesus' pitiable condition would elicit some measure of compassion from the elders and the people. But it was not to be.

Response: Jesus, the power of darkness was at its height in Your Passion. Still You were not afraid. Help me to follow Your example always.

Hail Mary

• *Then he handed him over to them to be crucified.* –John 19:16

Meditation: Judas handed Jesus over to the guards, who handed Him over to the religious leaders, who handed Him over to Pilate, who handed Him over to be crucified. In all this, Jesus was as a lamb led to the slaughter—for us.

Response: Jesus, bring me with You as You prepare to take up Your cross and walk the lonely road to Calvary.

Hail Mary

• *I gave my back to those who beat me, /*
my cheeks to those who plucked my beard. –Isaiah 50:6

Meditation: Jesus freely gave up His body to men who cared nothing for Him because He cared so deeply for them—and us.

Response: Jesus, You offered Yourself for me, enduring a pain that would pass away so I can enjoy an eternity that will not.

Hail Mary

• *My face I did not shield /*
from buffets and spitting. –Isaiah 50:6

Meditation: You know how much it hurts to be slapped in the face? Think of the abuse to which Jesus submitted Himself, as prophesied centuries earlier by the prophet Isaiah.

Response: Jesus, I react so quickly when I am hurt in any way. Please help me to remain in Your peace and respond more like You.

Hail Mary

Glory Be

Jesus Carries the Cross

In total surrender to His Father's Will, Jesus embraces the cross and bears it through Jerusalem's narrow and strident streets. In the faces of the shouting and jostling crowd He sees hate, rage, and disgust. Saddened but resolute, Jesus keeps going, toward His final end.

Although our crosses sometimes seem unbearable, God will never allow us to be tested beyond our ability to endure. He will always make a way. He is the God that heals and delivers us!

Our Father

• *It was preparation day for Passover, and it was about noon...So they took Jesus, and carrying the cross himself he went out to what is called the Place of the Skull, in Hebrew, Golgotha.* –John 19:14, 16-17

Meditation: As the temple priests prepare to sacrifice the Passover lambs, Jesus resolutely takes up His cross and sets out for Calvary.

Response: Lord Jesus, You freely laid down Your life for us. May we freely follow You through death to life.

Hail Mary

• *As they led him away they took hold of a certain Simon, a Cyrenian, who was coming in from the country; and after laying the cross on him, they made him carry it behind Jesus.*
–Luke 23:26

Meditation: Tradition holds that Simon, although initially compelled to bear the cross, later converted, and, with his whole family, followed Christ into the Kingdom.

Response: Jesus, at first our crosses seem heavy and unbearable. In time we realize that they are suited perfectly for us, and are given to bring us to You.

Hail Mary

• *Then he said to all, "If anyone wishes to come after me, he must deny himself,"* –Luke 9:23

Meditation: When two walk together, one must lead. Let us not only call Jesus Lord, but also do as He says.

Response: Change my heart, O God; Make me more like Jesus.

Hail Mary

• *"and take up his cross daily and follow me."* –Luke 9:23

Meditation: Just as Simon followed behind Jesus, so we are called daily to put on the yoke of Jesus, casting all our cares upon Him, and to follow Him on the road to ultimate victory!

Response: Lord, today is a new day. Forgetting what lies behind me, I press on behind You, to enter the Kingdom.

Hail Mary

- *A large crowd of people followed Jesus, including many women who mourned and lamented him.* –Luke 23:27

Meditation: Jesus had entered Jerusalem a week earlier amidst great rejoicing; He departs it now in mourning. *Sic transit gloria mundi!*

Response: Jesus, help me to deal wisely with both praise and humiliation. You are my Joy, O Lord, and my one desire!

Hail Mary

- *Jesus turned to them and said, "Daughters of Jerusalem, do not weep for me; weep instead for yourselves and for your children."* –Luke 23:28

Meditation: Jesus came unto His own, but they did not receive Him. This was the real tragedy.

Response: Lord, forgive me for the times I have not received You or those You put in my life. Help me open wide the doors to Christ!

Hail Mary

- *"If these things are done when the wood is green what will happen when it is dry?"* –Luke 23:31

Meditation: If one who was innocent suffered so, how would the guilty fare? Jesus thus invited the women of Jerusalem to believe in Him and find salvation.

Response: Lord, I prefer not to notice the suffering of the world. Help me to prevent and alleviate affliction where possible through Your Spirit of love.

Hail Mary

• He was spurned and avoided by men, / a man of suffering, accustomed to infirmity, / One of those from whom men hide their faces, / spurned, and we held him in no esteem.
–Isaiah 53:3

Meditation: Isaiah prophesies the rejection and abhorrence of the man of sorrows, a man held in no esteem.

Response: Lord, when people avoid or overlook me, I feel unnoticed and slighted. Yet You were spurned, despised, and rejected. Help me, Jesus, to seek only Your approval.

Hail Mary

• We had all gone astray like sheep, / each following his own way; / But the LORD laid upon him / the guilt of us all.
–Isaiah 53:6

Meditation: All of us have wandered off the path, down the dark, steep ravines of life. Our Shepherd has borne our guilt, and faithfully leads us home.

Response: O Good Shepherd, You did not run from us when the wolf came, but You bore our burdens gladly on the lonely road to Calvary. Thank You, dearest Friend!

Hail Mary

• Though he was harshly treated, he submitted / and opened not his mouth; / Like a lamb led to the slaughter / or a sheep before the shearers, / he was silent and opened not his mouth.
–Isaiah 53:7

Meditation: Jesus suffered in silence for the sake of us all.

Response: Lord, help me like You, to suffer in silence, trusting in Your mighty deliverance.

Hail Mary

Glory Be

The Crucifixion

The Good Shepherd climbs the tree of life to rescue His lost sheep, to reopen heaven's gates and give us a second chance at Paradise. Jesus thirsts for us to be with Him, reunited with His Father in the Kingdom prepared for us from the foundation of the world.

We stand with Mary at the foot of the Cross, "to enter with her into the depths of God's love for man and to experience all its life-giving power." –Pope Saint John Paul II

Our Father

• *There they crucified him, and with him two others, one on either side, with Jesus in the middle. –John 19:18*

Meditation: Crucifixion, a most painful and humiliating death, was reserved for the most serious of criminals. In taking upon Himself the enormity of our sin, Jesus took also the enormity of our punishment.

Response: Jesus, You accepted crucifixion out of love for me. Help me to live out of love for You.

Hail Mary

• *[Then Jesus said, "Father, forgive them, they know not what they do."]* –Luke 23:34

Meditation: Jesus pulled Himself up on His wounded hands so He could forgive us, and even excuse us, for our outrage against Him.

Response: Jesus, your great love astounds me. You did this for me. What can I do for You?

Hail Mary

• *Standing by the cross of Jesus were his mother and his mother's sister, Mary the wife of Clopas, and Mary of Magdala.* –John 19:25

Meditation: Only the bravest ventured near Jesus in His agony on the Cross. Their great love overcame their great fear.

Response: O Lord, You are the Love that overcomes my fear. Give me the strength to love You today, especially when You appear in the distressing disguise of someone in need.

Hail Mary

• *When Jesus saw his mother and the disciple there whom he loved, he said to his mother, "Woman, behold, your son."* –John 19:26

Meditation: From the Cross, Jesus gave Mary a gift and a mission: "Behold your children! Mother My brothers and sisters, and bring them into the Kingdom."

Response: Mary, I am all yours—*Totus Tuus!* Sweet Heart of Mary, be my salvation.

Hail Mary

• Then he said to the disciple, "Behold, your mother."
And from that hour the disciple took her into his home.
—John 19:27

Meditation: Jesus gave John an incredible gift and a mission as well: "Behold your Mother! Honor and care for her as your own."

Response: Dear Jesus, You gave me Your mother to be my mother! Thank You! May I always make a home for Mary in my heart.

Hail Mary

• And about three o'clock Jesus cried out in a loud voice, "Eli, Eli, lema sabachthani?" which means, "My God, my God, why have you forsaken me?" —Matthew 27:46

Meditation: At the climax of His suffering, Jesus cried out the first words of Psalm 22 —not a cry of despair, but a hymn of hope. Yes, He was in great agony. But no, He did not give up!

Response: O Jesus, forgive me for the many times I've yielded to pressure under trial. Give me the strength to praise You in times of trouble, for the help that is on its way!

Hail Mary

• After this, aware that everything was now finished, in order that the scripture might be fulfilled, Jesus said, "I thirst."
—John 19:28

Meditation: Jesus thirsted desperately, yet His great heart begged for more souls to repent and return to His Father.

Response: Jesus, You have one passion: to bring us all to heaven, our true home, to live with Your Father, Your Spirit, and You, forever. O Lord, take my hand, and may I bring others with me!

Hail Mary

• *When Jesus had taken the wine, he said, "It is finished."*
  –John 19:30

Meditation: After three hours of agony stretched out on the Cross, Jesus cried out, *"Tetelestai!"* —"Paid in full!" The work of our salvation was accomplished, the atonement was made, and Jesus had won!

Response: O Jesus, when I am tempted to despair because of my sin and weakness, let me trust in Your finished work on the Cross. You are the Victor, and I am eternally grateful.

Hail Mary

• *Jesus cried out in a loud voice, "Father, into your hands I commend my spirit"; and when he had said this he breathed his last.* –Luke 23:46

Meditation: As a little boy, Jesus had learned the psalms at Mary's knee. Now in His moment of death, from deep within the little boy cries out, "Into Your hands, Daddy, into Your hands, I surrender myself. Take me home with You, take me home!"

Response: O Jesus, I will never really understand just how much it cost You to save me. All I ask for is the grace to make it count.

Hail Mary

• *And he shall take away the sins of many, / and win pardon for their offenses.* –Isaiah 53:12

Meditation: In the end, all we can ever keep is Jesus and His love. And the only way to keep them, is to give them away.

Response: O Jesus, You died to give me new life. Let me live now for You. Into *Your* hands, O Lord, I commend my spirit.

Hail Mary

Glory Be

The Glorious Mysteries

The Resurrection of Jesus

"The contemplation of Christ's face cannot stop at the image of the Crucified One. He is the risen one!"
–Pope Saint John Paul II

Somewhere in the night, Jesus steps out of the grave with the fire of victory in His heart and an unconquerable joy in His soul. He has triumphed! Although the Scriptures are silent, surely He visits first His mother, first among His disciples. Jesus visits us as well, now and at the hour of our death, to bring us to Himself forever.

Our Father

On the first day of the week, Mary of Magdala came to the tomb early in the morning, while it was still dark, and saw the stone removed from the tomb. –John 20:1

Meditation: Mary and the other women journey at dawn to the tomb, to be greeted with the most astounding event in history: Jesus is risen from the dead!

Response: Lord Jesus, help me to seek You faithfully, even when it is most difficult. Thus will I receive You, my greatest reward.

Hail Mary

• While they were puzzling over this, behold, two men in dazzling garments appeared to them… . They said to them, "Why do you seek the living one among the dead?" –Luke 24:4-5

Meditation: Why do we seek the Living One among those dead in faith, dead in sin, or hardened of heart? Jesus, the Lion of Judah, calls us to Himself!

Response: O Jesus, forgive me for turning to lifeless idols of pleasure, power, and possessions, while You, the Risen One, invite me instead to receive the fullness of life.

Hail Mary

• When Simon Peter arrived…he went into the tomb and saw the burial cloths… .Then the other disciple also went in, and he saw and believed. –John 20:6-8

Meditation: Peter and John, witnesses of Jesus' suffering and death, were the first apostles to behold the empty tomb. Peter investigated; John saw and believed.

Response: Lord Jesus, many times I have been slow to believe. Please forgive me and call me deeper into the adventure of discovering You.

Hail Mary

• But Mary stayed outside the tomb weeping… .She turned around and saw Jesus there, but did not know it was Jesus. –John 20:11, 14

Meditation: Mary Magdalene wept inconsolably in her 'loss' of Jesus—and did not recognize Him standing before her!

Response: O Jesus, how often have I not recognized You in the persons and situations I encounter? Help me to see with new eyes.

Hail Mary

- *Jesus said to her, "Mary!" She turned and said to him in Hebrew, "Rabbouni," which means Teacher.* –John 20:16

Meditation: No one can speak our name like Jesus. When the Savior calls, let us answer Him with our whole heart.

Response: O Jesus, gentle Shepherd, I long to hear Your voice. Speak only the word, and I shall be healed.

Hail Mary

- *Jesus said to her, "Go to my brothers and tell them, 'I am going to my Father and your Father, to my God and your God.'"* –John 20:17

Meditation: Jesus commissions Mary as apostle to the apostles. The curse of the Fall is lifted—Jesus' Father is our Father, and His God is our God. We're back in the family again!

Response: Jesus, You call me Your brother, Your sister, Your friend. Praise God! O Father, I run into Your waiting arms!

Hail Mary

- *Now that very day two of them were going to…Emmaus… . And it happened that while they were conversing and debating, Jesus himself drew near and walked with them.* –Luke 24:13-15

Meditation: Although with us always, the Risen Lord draws near at the most unexpected times and in unexpected ways, especially in the Eucharist, His presence *par excellence.*

Response: O Lord, help me to recognize You today however You may come into my life. "Stay with us Lord, for it is nearly evening!"

Hail Mary

• He interpreted to them… the scriptures… . Then they said to each other, "Were not our hearts burning [within us] while he spoke to us on the way…?" –Luke 24:27, 32

Meditation: As Jesus opened the minds of His disciples to His Word, their burning hearts bore witness to the Messiah!

Response: Lord Jesus, only You can touch and warm us in the depths of our hearts. As Peter said so long ago, "Lord, to whom shall we go? You alone have the words of eternal life."

Hail Mary

• For you will not abandon me to Sheol, / nor let your faithful servant see the pit. –Psalm 16:10

Meditation: A thousand years before Christ, King David declared this promise, and Peter applies it to Jesus in his first sermon: **It was impossible for death to hold the Messiah!**

Response: Risen Lord, if I follow You, You will not abandon me to the nether world, nor allow me to suffer eternal corruption.

Hail Mary

• "I am the resurrection and the life; whoever believes in me, even if he dies, will live, and everyone who lives and believes in me will never die." –John 11:25-26

Meditation: Jesus, the Life that will never die, has definitively conquered sin, death, and the devil. Praise God!

Response: O Jesus, thank You for saving me from death! I receive today Your Resurrection power, power to abide in You and to live a life worthy of You now and forever. Alleluia!

Hail Mary

Glory Be

The Ascension of the Lord

After His Resurrection, Jesus encourages His disciples and builds up their faith. He blesses them with peace, grace, and strength to carry out His mission. His words return to mind: *"And if I go and prepare a place for you, I will come back again and take you to myself, so that where I am you also may be."* –John 14:3

Jesus is present to us in His Church, Word, and Sacraments, especially the Eucharist. Do I set my mind on the things that are above, where He is?

Our Father

• *He presented himself alive to them by many proofs after he had suffered, appearing to them during forty days and speaking about the kingdom of God.* –Acts 1:3

Meditation: Jesus knew His disciples would struggle in believing the Resurrection. He took time to encourage them and prepare them for their mission.

Response: O Lord, You patiently prepare me for my mission as well. Help me to be at peace with myself and others as You teach us day by day.

Hail Mary

*• He said to them, "These are my words that I spoke to you…
that everything written about me in the law of Moses and in the
prophets and psalms must be fulfilled."* –Luke 24:44

Meditation: God never does anything halfway. That's why His timetable is often different than ours. Jesus fulfilled *all* the Scriptures.

Response: O God, You have given me many and great promises in your Word. Help me to rely faithfully on Your Word and trust You to work everything out for the good.

Hail Mary

*• "Thus it is written that the Messiah would suffer and rise from
the dead on the third day,"* –Luke 24:46

Meditation: We must go through the Cross to come to the Resurrection. Thank God, Jesus has tasted death for us all!

Response: O Jesus, You never allow us to be tempted beyond our ability to endure. We rejoice even in our trials, hopeful of the Resurrection.

Hail Mary

*• "and that repentance, for the forgiveness of sins, would be
preached in his name to all the nations, beginning from
Jerusalem."* –Luke 24:47

Meditation: Jesus has a mission for His disciples, both then and now!

Response: O God, help me today to bring Your Good News to others; please bring all to salvation.

Hail Mary

- *"But you will receive power when the holy Spirit comes upon you, and you will be my witnesses in Jerusalem, throughout Judea and Samaria, and to the ends of the earth."* –Acts 1:8

Meditation: Jesus restores to us the presence and the power of almighty God. Now we can be *His* witnesses.

Response: O God, You promised in Genesis to restore us to Yourself. Send forth Your Spirit and renew the face of the earth!

Hail Mary

- *"And behold, I am with you always, until the end of the age."* –Matthew 28:20

Meditation: Like a father comforting his children at bedtime, Jesus assures us He will never leave us nor forsake us. After all, He is Emmanuel—God *with* us.

Response: O Jesus, I sometimes feel far from You. Yet I put my trust in You, that You are with me now and will be forever. Only in You is my soul at rest.

Hail Mary

- *When he had said this, as they were looking on, he was lifted up, and a cloud took him from their sight.* –Acts 1:9

Meditation: God's cloud of glory protected the Israelites in the Exodus, guided them in the desert, and filled their temple in Jerusalem. God's glory overshadowed Jesus in His Transfiguration and now lifts Him up into heaven.

Response: O Jesus, let your Father's cloud of glory overshadow all who are sick, tempted, or troubled this day. Spirit of the Living God, fall afresh on us!

Hail Mary

• *"Men of Galilee, why are you standing there looking at the sky? This Jesus...will return in the same way as you have seen him going into heaven."* –Acts 1:11

Meditation: Jesus' body is gone. His Spirit remains. Christ has no body now but ours, and there is work to be done.

Response: O Lord, may I fulfill Your Will for me, and make ready Your return.

Hail Mary

• *They did him homage and then returned to Jerusalem with great joy, and they were continually in the temple praising God.* –Luke 24:52-53

Meditation: Jesus brought great joy at His coming and at His departure. Glory to God in the Highest!

Response: O Lord, help me to praise You in all things. You are now in heaven, where you live forever to intercede for us.

Hail Mary

• *The LORD says to you, my lord: / "Take your throne at my right hand, / while I make your enemies your footstool."* –Psalm 110:1

Meditation: David prophesies of a Messianic King who would be both Lord and Son. Jesus takes His throne as His Father dismantles His enemies in every age.

Response: Lord Jesus, I rejoice in Your finished work; I am available to do Your Will on earth.

Hail Mary

Glory Be

The Descent of the Holy Spirit

Mary and the disciples pray as Jesus had instructed them. Early Pentecost morning, a noise like a strong driving wind fills the whole house and tongues of fire rest on all. Filled with the Holy Spirit, the infant Church goes forth in power, for the Comforter has come!

Let us ask the Spirit to fill us with His gifts, that we may produce fruits of love, joy, peace, patience, kindness, generosity, faithfulness, gentleness, and self-control.

Our Father

• *All these devoted themselves with one accord to prayer, together with some women, and Mary the mother of Jesus, and his brothers.* –Acts 1:14

Meditation: Through her quiet, contemplative presence, Mary led the disciples as they fervently sought the risen Lord.

Response: O Lord, You have commanded us to pray always; Help me, with Mary, to obey.

Hail Mary

• *When the time for Pentecost was fulfilled,*
they were all in one place together. –Acts 2:1

Meditation: Pentecost was the Jewish Harvest feast commemorating the giving of the Law on Mount Sinai. The disciples were united as they waited upon the Lord.

Response: Lord, I surrender to Your plans and timetable for me. Help me to dwell in unity with all who seek Your Spirit.

Hail Mary

• *And suddenly there came from the sky a noise like a strong driving wind, and it filled the entire house in which they were.*
–Acts 2:2

Meditation: God gave the Law on Mount Sinai in thunder, fire, and a loud trumpet blast. The Holy Spirit comes in wind and fire with the New Law at Pentecost.

Response: Lord God, You come in power to suffuse my entire being. O Holy Spirit, fall afresh on me!

Hail Mary

• *Then there appeared to them tongues as of fire,*
which parted and came to rest on each one of them. –Acts 2:3

Meditation: Jesus fulfills His promise to cast fire upon the earth as His Spirit births the Church, igniting it with passion to bring the world to His Father!

Response: O Lord, Your fire purifies and energizes me. Send forth Your Spirit, and renew the face of the earth.

Hail Mary

• *And they were all filled with the holy Spirit and began to speak in different tongues, as the Spirit enabled them to proclaim.*
–Acts 2:4

Meditation: *All* the disciples were filled with the *one* Spirit. *United* in heart, they proclaimed the wonders of the Lord.

Response: Lord, in my Baptism and Confirmation You filled me with Your Spirit. Help me speak Your Word of love through my deeds this day.

Hail Mary

• *Then Peter stood up with the Eleven…and proclaimed…"You who are Jews, indeed all of you staying in Jerusalem. This is what was spoken through the prophet Joel:"* –Acts 2:14, 16

Meditation: Peter, now the courageous Rock, preaches that God is at this *very* moment sending down His long-awaited Spirit!

Response: O God, long have we waited for You. In Your mercy, fill us again with the power of Your Holy Spirit!

Hail Mary

• *" 'It will come to pass in the last days,' God says, / 'that I will pour out a portion of my spirit / upon all flesh.' "*
–Acts 2:17

Meditation: Peter, quoting from the prophet Joel, proclaims that God is pouring out His promised Spirit for a special reason: to invite all to salvation.

Response: O Lord, the last days have stretched from Pentecost unto this day, as You mercifully call your children to Yourself. Help me to proclaim Your good news to someone today.

Hail Mary

> • " 'and it shall be that everyone shall be saved
> who calls on the name of the Lord.' " –Acts 2:21

Meditation: *The Spirit prepares men and goes out to them...to draw them to Christ. ...He makes present the mystery of Christ, supremely in the Eucharist...to bring them into communion with God. –Catechism of the Catholic Church, par. 737*

Response: O Lord, our ultimate goal is union with You. Help all of us to call on Your name and be saved!

Hail Mary

> • *Those who accepted his message were baptized,
> and about three thousand persons were added that day.*
> –Acts 2:41

Meditation: *"Pentecost...reveals the face of the Church as a family gathered together with Mary, enlivened by the powerful outpouring of the Spirit and ready for the mission of evangelization." –Pope Saint John Paul II*

Response: O Lord, Your Spirit makes us a family of love, warmth, and reconciliation. Help us continue to grow in You.

Hail Mary

> • *I will give you a new heart and place a new spirit within you,
> taking from your bodies your stony hearts and giving you
> natural hearts. –Ezekiel 36:26*

Meditation: God fulfills Ezekiel's prophecy as He enters into a *new* covenant with the *New* Israel: the Church.

Response: O Lord, please take away my hardened heart today, and give me a heart of love. Amen.

Hail Mary

Glory Be

The Assumption of Mary

The Church teaches that Mary, the Mother of Jesus, was taken up body and soul into heaven after the completion of her earthly life. Because of her Immaculate Conception, Mary was freed from the consequences of Original Sin. According to Pope Saint John Paul II, Mary would enjoy "beforehand, by a unique privilege, the destiny reserved for all the just at the resurrection of the dead." Mary is thus both a sign of what heaven holds for us and a Mother to help us get there.

Our Father

• *My lover speaks; he says to me, / "Arise, my beloved, my beautiful one, / and come!"* –Song of Songs 2:10

Meditation: After the Ascension of Jesus, Mary lived with Saint John and guided the infant Church. Even so, her heart was always with her Son, who now calls His Mother home to Himself.

Response: O Mary, I can only imagine your longing for Jesus! Help me to also desire only heaven, with Jesus and you, forever.

Hail Mary

- *"For see, the winter is past, / the rains are over and gone."*
  –Song of Songs 2:11

Meditation: Mary worked hard all her life, in every way. She endured the winter of sorrow and the rain of tears. Now the springtime has come!

Response: O Lord, many are our trials in this life, but out of them all You will deliver us. Preserve me, for in You I place my trust.

Hail Mary

- *"Blessed are you, daughter, by the Most High God, above all the women on earth."* –Judith 13:18

Meditation: Indeed Mary was blessed by God, to fulfill a task only she could do.

Response: We too have been and are now being blessed by our generous God. Help me, O Lord, to fulfill my vocation through Mary's intercession.

Hail Mary

- *"Your deed of hope will never be forgotten by those who tell of the might of God."* –Judith 13:19

Meditation: Every generation has honored Mary, the Mother of Jesus and spiritual Mother of us all. She is the new Eve!

Response: Thank you, Mary, for your *Fiat*—your *Yes*—to God, which allowed us to receive so great a Redeemer.

Hail Mary

- *"You are the glory of Jerusalem, / the surpassing joy of Israel; / You are the splendid boast of our people."* –Judith 15:9

Meditation: The lovely young lady from Nazareth has become the Mother of the Church! Truly Mary is the glory of God's people.

Response: Our hearts are full as we fly to you O Mary, "our tainted nature's solitary boast." *–William Wordsworth, The Virgin*

Hail Mary

- *"Arise, LORD, come to your resting place, / you and your majestic ark."* –Psalm 132:8

Meditation: The Church sees Mary, who carried the Son of God in her womb, as the new Ark of the Covenant.

Response: King David brought the Ark to Jerusalem, but the Son of David brought Mary, body, and soul, into heaven! Bring us also home, O Lord, at our journey's end.

Hail Mary

- *Then God's temple in heaven was opened, and the ark of his covenant could be seen in the temple. There were flashes of lightning, rumblings, and peals of thunder, an earthquake, and a violent hailstorm.* –Revelation 11:19

Meditation: The Ark of God's Covenant is in His temple: in her Assumption, Mary takes her rightful place in heaven.

Response: Mary, your profound humility on earth is matched only by your exaltation in heaven. Help me to keep my eyes always upon Jesus.

Hail Mary

• *And Mary said: / "My soul proclaims the greatness of the Lord; / my spirit rejoices in God my savior."* –Luke 1:46-47

Meditation: Mary praises God for His past, present, and future work in her, and in His Church, of which she is the model.

Response: O Lord, through the example of Mary, first among the disciples, we proclaim your greatness and rejoice in Your salvation.

Hail Mary

• *"For he has looked upon his handmaid's lowliness; / behold, from now on will all ages call me blessed."* –Luke 1:48

Meditation: God seeks not our *ability*, but our *availability*. In her humility, the grace-filled Mary caught the eye of God.

Response: Blessed are you, O Mary, now in heaven forever with your Son! Help me to serve as you did.

Hail Mary

• *"The Mighty One has done great things for me, / and holy is his name."* –Luke 1:49

Meditation: After a life of obedient love, God brings Mary, body and soul, into the fullness of His Kingdom forever.

Response: O God, Mary is our example, our model, and most of all, our Mother! Through her intercession, You will also do great things for us, for holy is Your name.

Hail Mary

Glory Be

The Coronation of Mary

"God is preparing a new dwelling place and a new earth where justice will abide, and whose blessedness will answer and surpass all the longings for peace which spring up in the human heart." —Pope Benedict XVI

In this final mystery, "Mary shines forth as Queen of the Angels and Saints, the anticipation and the supreme realization of the eschatological state of the Church." –*Pope Saint John Paul II, The Rosary of the Virgin Mary*

Our Father

• *Who is this that comes forth like the dawn, /
as beautiful as the moon, as resplendent as the sun, /
as awe-inspiring as bannered troops?*
–Song of Songs 6:10

Meditation: Mary, symbol of the Church, steps forward to receive her reward and begin her reign.

Response: O Mary, beautiful in spirit, soul, and body, you cooperated fully with God's grace. Help me, like you, to respond to His grace today.

Hail Mary

*• All glorious is the king's daughter as she enters, /
her raiment threaded with gold. –Psalm 45:14*

Meditation: As Mary enters heaven, her golden raiment represents her good deeds. She is daughter and Mother, disciple and Queen.

Response: Lord, our deeds will accompany us into Your presence. Help us to serve You with a cheerful, humble heart!

Hail Mary

*• In embroidered apparel she is led to the king. /
The maids of her train are presented to the king. –Psalm 45:15*

Meditation: Can you imagine the joy in heaven as Mary is presented to God, in the company of all the angels and saints?

Response: O Jesus, as I endure the trials and temptations of earth, help me remember that someday I will stand before Your heavenly throne. May Mary be with me now, and then.

Hail Mary

*• A great sign appeared in the sky, a woman clothed with the
sun, with the moon under her feet, and on her head a crown of
twelve stars. –Revelation 12:1*

Meditation: Mary shines forth in all her splendor crowned as Queen of the Church, which is born of Israel and founded on the apostles.

Response: O Mary, you are all humble yet most powerful. Pray for us, O Holy Mother of God, that we may be made worthy of the promises of Christ.

Hail Mary

• She gave birth to a son, a male child, destined to rule all the nations with an iron rod. Her child was caught up to God and his throne. –Revelation 12:5

Meditation: Psalm 2 speaks of the Messiah who will rule all nations with an iron rod, symbol of His authority. As Queen Mother, Mary reigns with her Son.

Response: O God, You are our Father, and we are your children. Help us to serve You with reverence and awe, and take refuge always in You.

Hail Mary

*• I rejoice heartily in the LORD, /
in my God is the joy of my soul.* –Isaiah 61:10

Meditation: In her Magnificat, reminiscent of Isaiah's ode, Mary praises the God whose word is true and whose reign most certainly will come. Joy is the sign of His victory!

Response: O Lord, I too rejoice with Mary in all circumstances. Thank You that we have a King *and* a Queen to aid us on earth!

Hail Mary

*• For he has clothed me with a robe of salvation, /
and wrapped me in a mantle of justice.* –Isaiah 61:10

Meditation: God clothes Mary, the new Eve, in a robe of salvation and a mantle of righteousness, signs of His favor and loving provision.

Response: O God, I put on my spiritual armor today, as described in Ephesians 6:10-17. Thank you for clothing us also with Your favor and protection!

Hail Mary

• Like a bridegroom adorned with a diadem, /
like a bride bedecked with her jewels. –Isaiah 61:10

Response: God, who is never outdone in generosity, crowns
Mary as Queen of Heaven and earth, who "dedicates herself
totally to the work of salvation." *–Pope Saint John Paul II*

Hail Mary

• If we have died with him we shall also live with him; /
if we persevere we shall also reign with him.
–2 Timothy 2:11-12

Meditation: Saint Paul asserts that this saying is trustworthy,
and indeed it is. Mary is the forerunner of all who seek to follow
Christ, through His death, to a like resurrection.

Response: Dear God, I want to follow you, like Mary did. I am
weak and I fail often. Help me to persevere to the end, to be
faithful unto death, that I might receive the crown of life.

Hail Mary

• The Spirit and the bride say, "Come." Let the hearer say,
"Come." Let the one who thirsts come forward, and the one who
wants it receive the gift of life-giving water. –Revelation 22:17

Meditation: Jesus and Mary urge us to repent and be converted,
to come to the Font of living water, and receive eternal life.

Response: O Mary, you are our Mother and Queen. Show unto
us the blessed fruit of thy womb, Jesus, now and forever. Amen!

Hail Mary

Glory Be

Prayers After the Rosary

Hail, Holy Queen

Hail, Holy Queen, Mother of Mercy,
Our life, our sweetness, and our hope!
To thee do we cry, poor banished
children of Eve; to thee do we send
up our sighs, mourning and weeping
in this valley of tears. Turn then,
most gracious advocate, thine eyes
of mercy toward us; and after this
our exile show unto us the blessed
fruit of thy womb, Jesus; O clement,
O loving, O sweet Virgin Mary.

V-Pray for us, O holy mother of God,
R-That we may be made worthy of the promises of Christ.

Let us pray: O God, whose only-begotten Son, by His life, death
and resurrection, has purchased for us the rewards of eternal life;
grant, we beseech Thee, that, meditating upon these mysteries of
the Most Holy Rosary of the Blessed Virgin Mary, we may
imitate what they contain and obtain what they promise, through
the same Christ our Lord. Amen.

Memorare

Remember, O most gracious Virgin Mary, that never was it
known, that any one who fled thy protection, implored thy
help or sought thy intercession, was left unaided. Inspired by this
confidence, I fly unto thee, O Virgin of virgins my Mother; to
thee do I come, before thee I stand, sinful and sorrowful. O
Mother of the Word Incarnate, despise not my petitions, but in
thy mercy hear and answer me. Amen.

Litany of the Blessed Virgin Mary

V- Lord, have mercy. **R- Christ, have mercy.**

V- Lord, have mercy.

V- Jesus, hear us. **R- Jesus, graciously hear us.**

V- God the Father of Heaven, **R- have mercy on us.**

V- God the Son, Redeemer of the world, **R- have mercy on us.**

V- God the Holy Spirit, **R- have mercy on us.**

V- Holy Trinity, One God, **R- have mercy on us.**

R- Pray for us

Holy Mary,
Holy Mother of God,
Holy Virgin of virgins,
Mother of Christ,
Mother of divine grace,
Mother most pure,
Mother most chaste,
Mother inviolate,
Mother undefiled,
Mother most amiable,
Mother most admirable,
Mother of good counsel,
Mother of our Creator,
Mother of our Redeemer,
Mother of the Church,
Virgin most prudent,
Virgin most venerable,
Virgin most renowned,
Virgin most powerful,
Virgin most merciful,
Virgin most faithful,

R- Pray for us

Mirror of justice,
Seat of wisdom,
Cause of our joy,
Spiritual vessel,
Vessel of honor,
Singular vessel of devotion,
Mystical rose,
Tower of David,
Tower of ivory,
House of gold,
Ark of the Covenant,
Gate of Heaven,
Morning star,
Health of the sick,
Refuge of sinners,
Comforter of the afflicted,
Help of Christians,
Queen of angels,
Queen of patriarchs,
Queen of prophets,
Queen of apostles,
Queen of martyrs,
Queen of confessors,
Queen of virgins,
Queen of all saints,
Queen conceived without original sin,
Queen assumed into Heaven,
Queen of the most holy Rosary,
Queen of families,
Queen of peace,

V- Lamb of God, You take away the sins of the world,
R- Spare us, O Lord.
V- Lamb of God, You take away the sins of the world,
R- Graciously hear us, O Lord.
V- Lamb of God, You take away the sins of the world,
R- Have mercy on us.
V- Pray for us, O Holy Mother of God.
R- That we may be made worthy of the promises of Christ.

Let us pray: Grant, we beseech You, O Lord God, that we Your servants may enjoy perpetual health of mind and body and by the glorious intercession of the Blessed Mary, ever Virgin, be delivered from present sorrow and enjoy eternal happiness. Through Christ, Our Lord. Amen.

Magnificat

And Mary said:
"My soul proclaims the greatness of the Lord;
  my spirit rejoices in God my savior.
For he has looked upon his handmaid's lowliness;
  behold, from now on will all ages call me blessed.
The Mighty One has done great things for me,
  and holy is his name.
His mercy is from age to age
  to those who fear him.
He has shown might with his arm,
  dispersed the arrogant of mind and heart.
He has thrown down the rulers from their thrones
  but lifted up the lowly.
The hungry he has filled with good things;
  the rich he has sent away empty.
He has helped Israel his servant,
  remembering his mercy,
according to his promise to our fathers,
  to Abraham and to his descendants forever."

The Fatima Message and First Saturday Devotion

The Mother of God appeared at Fatima, Portugal, six times between May 13th and October 13th, 1917, to three shepherd children: Lucia, Jacinta and Francisco. Our Lady of the Rosary told the children that God had sent her with a message for every man, woman, and child. Coming at a time when civilization was torn asunder by war and violence, Mary promised that Heaven would grant peace to the world if her requests for prayer, reparation and consecration were heard and obeyed.

Mary warned that if people continued to disobey God's Will, they would suffer the consequences of war, hunger and persecution of the Church. She also prophesied that Russia would "spread her errors" of atheism and materialism across the earth. Our Lady repeatedly emphasized the necessity of praying the Rosary daily, of wearing the Brown Scapular, and of performing acts of reparation and sacrifice.

Mary also said, "I promise to help at the hour of death, with the graces needed for salvation, whoever on the First Saturday of five consecutive months shall:

• Confess and receive Communion
• Pray five decades of the Rosary
• Keep me company for fifteen minutes while meditating on the mysteries of the Rosary, with the intention of making reparation to me."

"O Queen of the Rosary...O dearest Mother, O Refuge of Sinners, O Sovereign Consoler of the Afflicted, may you be everywhere blessed, today and always, on earth and in heaven."
–Blessed Bartolo Longo